Charlie Charles
LIFE'S LESSONS LEARNT

Poems, Lyrics and Vivid Dreams

To Jackie
Thanks for all your
Support x

C. Barrett

PreeTa ✳ Press

Charlie's Story

My name is Charlie Barrett, I was born December 23rd
1966, my parents came over from Jamaica during the
Windrush period, my father worked as a manual labourer
before he was able to start his own business, we lived in
one of the most deprived areas of Bolton. On the street we
lived, there were Jamaican, Pakistani, Indian, Barbadian,
and English residents, the area was a real melting pot of
diversity. The social environment was not welcoming to
newcomers, and racism was at a substantial level where it
was the norm for passersby to verbally abuse people like
myself and their families.

Having to struggle for social integration and having a
continuous bravado mind-set, my only respite lay indoors
with my parents. They were my biggest influences in my
life, my biggest encouragers, I consumed their attention,
and was loved for who I was, never inferior because of the
colour of my skin or where I came from. They taught me
many lessons throughout my life that I find myself passing
on to my own children, "Manners maketh the man" and
"cleanliness is next to godliness", along with many more
quotes from my parents, more importantly, they questioned
me on my understanding of such truths.

My father was my biggest influence, he was a fantastic
story-teller. His life had been hard and he used his
experience to teach and guide me with affection. As an
infant his own father had died, which left his mother the

task of raising a family on her own in Jamaica, practically impossible at that time, her only option, to re marry. His step-father always subjected him to horrendous cruelty, of all his siblings he was the only one abused and neglected. In his early 20s he had the opportunity to go to America, for interviews and medical exams, he was fortunate enough that a friend was able to make sure he had clean clothes and his very first pair of real shoes, making him presentable for this opportunity. Before moving over to the UK he had made a mission to find this friend and thank him.

Poetry and song writing have been a huge factor in my life, being my personal and emotional safety net to deal with the issues in my life, helping me to process the traumas of racialism and being a second class citizen. Poetry and song writing also introduced me to a wonderful community of people like myself, and later allowed me to help young people process their traumas in a creative way.

Life experiences, through being, "different", have taught me many things allowing me to closely relate to young people I seek to help, no matter their creed. If I could find a creative way to guide them, giving them the tools they required to continue their journey as individuals with pride and confidence, I would take value from that. My aim is, and always will be to have a positive effect on young people and that they go away with the same encouragement and confidence that my parents instilled in me.

My dad used to tell me "It doesn't matter the relationship, you only need two elements for it to be successful, communication and compromise," and I have put this into practice in my life many times, instigating value with my time and my connections, which have become many. My father always said "Finding a true friend is as hard to find as a rocking horse droppings", finding true friends gives you the ability to move mountains together.

When I left school in 1983 I only had an art qualification, I didn't apply myself to any other subject because no other subjects appealed to me at the time.
I loved school but only the social aspect of it. I felt no pressure to get those qualifications as my father believed I would follow him into his driving tipper wagons business, but because I couldn't start that until I was 21 I spent years moving from dead-end-job to dead-end-job with no real hope for my future. I never really wanted to join my father's business but felt I would let him down if I didn't.

During this time, I stayed active with the local youths and even helped organise football matches and other activities for the local children. In this period, I would connect to all kinds of groups, black, Asian, white it didn't matter, I would connect with them and eventually bring them all together for football matches and other events. The time was busy with music and BBQ's providing a base for integration and inclusion, myself being the prominent instigator, this was a rare theme at the time, which opened the doors to unity in an environment where young people squabbled amongst themselves.

Shortly after, I met Hanif Ali, who was to become a future life friend and mentor, having similarities as a street kid with similar issues. His experience encouraged me to focus on my youth work and become qualified as an official youth worker. He assisted me to embrace formal education and to focus on counselling, assisting me with funding for books and supplies, but more importantly confidence. Without Hanif I would not have taken that first step being where I am today, helping people, especially those who are young, making positive change in my community which I continue today.

I greatly value Hanif as being my first mentor, his help has guided me to my second mentor, Denise Luczka, who was my tutor when I took my youth worker qualification. She recognised a natural ability to work with difficult and challenging young people, even though I believed I was a natural, she insisted on practical theory, understanding of the methods to work with young people. I got the bug for education and took on my counselling qualification, again Denise mentored me through this process. She managed a counselling agency 'The GAP' and gave me my first placement and office to begin counselling young people on a one-to-one basis, she also found me positions in local schools to counsel children on a one-to-one basis.

I eventually obtained my counselling diploma, and developed my own counselling service, "Cherry New Music Therapy".

In retrospect, the magnitude of young people with issues was alarming, every day I had an insight in what they were going through, receiving abuse and trauma, there weren't enough hours in the day to deal with the client group. Today, the same assistance for young people is more prevalent. In the last three years, young people and the abuse they face every day from social media and cyber-bullying has tripled the negative effect the young people of today feel. Budget cuts and lack of funding to services has been detrimental in supporting today's young people and it's not getting better. We are in crisis, and it is a disservice to our young people to not properly fund these services.

Everyday more young people struggle with their mental health issues. 'Cherry New Music Therapy' was very successful and over-subscribed, there were very few similar services in the north west with this delivery. Young people with mental health issues couldn't find the funding to access our services, this led me to look for other ways to deliver, which would be more easily accessible to those who needed it the most. Therefore, I created 'Harmony Youth Project' to widen the spectrum of services, initiatives that included art, dance, music, sport, etc. Allowing the children to see their full career, future opportunities and potential and be encouraged to overcome the barriers to help them pursue their dreams. It was through this work that in 2005 I became the winner of the 'Black and Asian Achievements Award', for my work with 'Harmony Youth Project', the first winner being Amir Khan.

The main focus of Harmony Youth Project has always been the children, their mental health and giving them the tools they need to maintain their mental health after they leave us. While I was running counselling sessions we would work with the client to convert our session notes to lyrics and process our interpretation of their struggles and make something positive and beautiful from it. The end result, the young person would receive a copy of the track and lyrics for the experience and lyrical content to remind them of the issues and problems they have managed to overcome.

Years ago I put together young people from various deprived estates and areas around Bolton and we formed 'The Blackout Crew' a musical group of young and talented people. We recorded their first album at the charity studio and the band were signed to major record label 'Clubland', they're videos were shown daily on MTV and inspired others from similar backgrounds to reach for their own dreams. So many adults who spent time with us at Harmony Youth Project as children have grown to have very successful careers in the creative arts, social work and youth work, etc. I'd like to believe the time they spent at the charity had a very positive influence and helped them achieve their ambitions.

In 2021 The Harmony youth project charity celebrated our 20-years anniversary. The early years were criticised with negative connotations, nobody believed a black man in Bolton who left school with nothing could instigate so much positive change. I had to work twice as hard as my counterparts, but I kept going with belief and optimism in memory of my dear father. We are still here strong and determined in getting stronger.

Thanking God

I'm not the most religious man in the world but I do believe there is a God. So first and foremost, I would like to thank God for my life and loves experiences, good and bad.

Thanking Diane

A message for my partner Diane, who was the inspiration and the muse for a large proportion of these poems. Through the sunshine and the storms. x

Contents

EIGHT DREAMS

She came to me crashing through the stars

With love's precision like an arrow, she pierced my heart

And from that day she filled my life with wonder

I really can't believe the power of this spell she's put me under

Everyday feels like a dream, so afraid I'll wake up, look around knowing in despair

That it's impossible to replace this life of love if you ever disappear

Just like when I hear your voice, it's such a heavenly sound

When I look deep into your eyes, I swear it makes my world go round

I can't recall any memories of my time when you weren't here with me

Loving you for a lifetime just isn't enough or even eternity

If I were granted one wish and just one wish alone

I'd make you my queen in a place that we'd call home

With all the love in your heart, your compassion, tenderness and grace

1

I'd know throughout all the universe there would be no better place

I'm going to give you some simple instructions to help you get through your day

So, settle down get comfortable, now listen to what I have to say

1, First things first, no need to panic, everything happens for a reason, what doesn't kill you makes you stronger

One day we'll all look back on this and laugh about the pressure we were put under

2, You need to try to find the positives, there are so many if you look hard enough, believe me what I say is true

Take this opportunity to do the things you never had time before to do

Write a book, learn to play guitar, spend quality time with your loved ones

Reflect upon some of your regrets, do things you maybe wish you'd done

3, Life for all of us goes so fast, let's just slow the madness down

Take some time appreciate the wonder all around

Things you take for granted, you walk by every day

You only tend to miss what's been destroyed or taken away

4, Make a promise to yourself, one you're sure to keep, live by the simple rule to change your life, all you sow you reap

5, Positivity and love really do make this crazy world we live in spin

Every man, woman and child should make love their new religion

Everybody's made mistakes done things they knew were wrong

Temptation is a constant cross we bare, we can't always be strong

Remember forgiveness is divine, God truly loves a trier

When this crisis finally ends, rise like a Phoenix from the fire

6, Forget conspiracy theories, forget trying to find the ones to blame

Let's all take this opportunity to try to change the game

Let's fight for our environment, end starvation, prejudice and war

Let's try to make a world for all our children to adore

7, Ignore the colour of someone's skin, or where they may come from

It's all about the rule of love, we all must live as one

If you want a better future, no more excuses, make a change

Let's write a brand new chapter in the book of life, let's turn another page

I know you think I'm crazy, but what I'm saying is quite easy for us all to do

If we all just come together, you'll be amazed what we can do

8, Whether you're a child, middle aged or a senior citizen

The fact is that we all must die, it's part of the master plan

Death gives us all a chance to see the difference that we have made

Black or white, rich or poor, a master or a slave

No one's escaping judgment day, I find great comfort knowing that

Let's not waste this fantastic opportunity, it's time for all of us to act

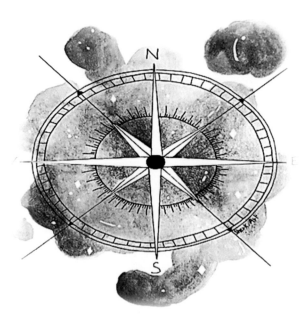

A HOUSE A HOME

I know I said it, but I really didn't mean it

Everybody told me that they saw it, I just didn't see it

Maybe it's true, love is blind

But this girl is making me lose my God damn mind

I'd do almost anything just to make her smile

I'd cross the largest desert, I'd swim across the Nile

I'd give her everything I have

I'd give her everything I own

I only have one wish from her

Please make this house a home

All my friends tell me I could do much better

They disapproved of her the very first time they met her

Yeah you know they told me right from the start

Sooner rather than later that girl, she'll break your heart

But like I fool I wouldn't listen

I said you don't know her like I do

But all the pain they predicted, everything they told me I regret was true

But I'd still give her everything I have

I'd give her everything I own

If she would grant me just one wish

Make this house a home

ALONE

There's only one sun, is the sun alone?
There's only one moon, is the moon alone?
I'd argue no for the sun serves everyone
The same said for the moon since time begun
They both measure time tide and our fate

The story has been written already, repent it's too late
So as I stare at my reflection what do I see?
A little boy lost like a ship in the sea

Afraid of my future from the pain of my past
So how do I change things when the die has been cast
Happiness isn't permanent, it's the fear that torments and
drags on

I'm just waiting for the rainbow when the dark clouds have
all gone
They say it's the hope that will kill you, but hope is all I
have left
I still believe courage strength and faith will get me out of
this mess

AND SO, IT WILL BE

The sun is God

The moon she's moody

The sea is spiteful

The sky is temporary

The stars are angels

The clouds are thoughts

The grass always giving

The earth a big plate

Every colour a clue

Each day a Gift

Time, the most precious commodity

Blood, the Roots Family

The future, a mystery already written

So, I say what will be, will be

BALANCE

As time goes by and I get older

Days go fast and people get colder

Dreams I held dear when I was young and care free

Have wilted and died like leaves from a tree

I stood and saw them lay flat on the ground

I heard the wind twirl them around and around

So why are my branches now laden with fruit?

It's the love from my leaves that replenished my roots

BOY

I put my feelings in a bottle
Screwed the cork tight on top
I threw the bottle in the sea
I thought the hurt would stop

But the sea was rough
And the storms were cruel
So lay loose my cork

That's when I had to face the truth
Find the strength to talk
When I looked inside the glass
All my lies came true

So I put a sail upon my heart
And came back home to you
The little boy who went to sea

I knew you'd understand
That when I finally reach your shore

This boy would be a man

BIRD STORY

I won't fly away

Don't squeeze me too tight you will crush my wings

Remember when I came to you my wings mangled, my

mind twisted, by cruel words from important, but

irresponsible people?

I love you so much you don't know

I love you so much, I try to fly your way to your destination

without question

Even though I know, in my heart of hearts

I know I can't do that, not without feeling

I need you to believe in me, for me to become truly free

Because no matter where I go, you're always with me

For I am just a man!

Who has inherited the weakness, curiosity, and ignorance

of every other man who walked before me?

Sometimes I see it in your eyes, the desperation for me to

change

But when I step closer I see myself in the mirror,

I would like to think the older I get the wiser I get, that's

why as every day goes by you become more beautiful

Not just to look at but to be around

And that feeling like a glow gets stronger and stronger

from you

So much so, I often fear it, because that glow is love and I

have felt that love before

A rage like the sun, it burned my wings and twisted my

mind, it sent me crashing to the ground and I cursed love

Until I realised if the sun had not caused me such pain, I

would never had found you.

BROKEN (bad man)

You should have left her alone

She was such a good girl but now she's broken

Why did you break her heart?

You should have put her on the right track

You should have left her alone

But instead you chose to lead her astray

Making promises you couldn't keep

Left her broken hearted, crying all alone at night

She couldn't sleep

Because you were always on the town

Playing around, you never gave her a second thought

Now this beautiful girl is walking around with a broken heart

You should have left her alone

Giving her a chance to find a good man

You should have given her a chance to heal her heart

But you chose to lead her astray

Yeah you just gave all her love away

She deserves much better

Better than a bad man

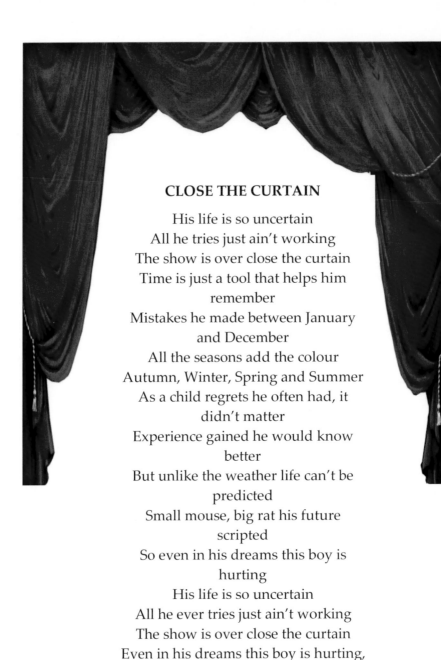

CLOSE THE CURTAIN

His life is so uncertain
All he tries just ain't working
The show is over close the curtain
Time is just a tool that helps him
remember
Mistakes he made between January
and December
All the seasons add the colour
Autumn, Winter, Spring and Summer
As a child regrets he often had, it
didn't matter
Experience gained he would know
better
But unlike the weather life can't be
predicted
Small mouse, big rat his future
scripted
So even in his dreams this boy is
hurting
His life is so uncertain
All he ever tries just ain't working
The show is over close the curtain
Even in his dreams this boy is hurting,

COLOURED FLOWERS

When I'm alone I often find

Like a spider disappointment creeps in my mind

Weaving a web of self-destruction

Until survival becomes my only function

Then one day in my bedsit cell

I saw a creature I thought from hell

In the corner of my dingy room

There shone a light brighter than the moon

It picked me up with love and affection

And showed me the world, through another dimension

Now coloured flowers block my view

Now my world is bright and new

Disappointments left behind

In the shadows of my mind

CROOKED FELLA

I never meant to hurt you girl

I never meant to make you cry

Didn't mean to desert you, deceive, abuse you or lie

Didn't mean to leave you every time you needed me near

I tried my best to keep my promises

But I was never quite sincere

I made excuses whenever I let you down

Suppose to take you out

Instead chose to play out

With my boys, acting the fool, with another girl on my arm in town

I didn't respect you, instead I'd neglect you

I took your love for granted

I just didn't give a damn

So why you're still with me, I just can't understand

You say one day, someday, you'll change your ways

So does that mean you'll be waiting for me years, months
or days?

So let me give you some sound advice

Prepare yourself for a real long wait

Coz I'm such a crooked kind of fella

I spent a lifetime trying to get straight

CROSSES

You're my cross I have to bare

The shame l have to wear, everywhere, I can't share

Like a coat five times too big that drowns me, surrounds me

Night and day there's no escaping it, excusing it, denying it, avoiding it

Like your DNA you just can't change it, exchange it

My destiny, my history, my only choice, was meant to be

Fact not fiction, hear me out

Ain't no cure, ain't no doubt

I'm sorry that's just the way it is

With this affliction I must live

Pray every day curse this life I live

I won't cast a shadow on my kids

I can't imagine anything worse than that

Can't allow them to see how I act

For the cross I carry, is my own

The weight of it is all I've known

I know one day I'll find the strength to shed my cross

That day I'll find the love I lost

CROSSES

DARE TO DREAM

Try never to rely on the unreliable

Constantly being let down becomes just unbearable

Don't be driven by hatred, make a beeline to love

Try to end every day with memories you can be proud of

Remember regrets are for those who have not dared to dream

Open your heart, your mind, make love supreme

Have you ever wondered what fear took away?

When you look back at your life, what would you do differently today?

If somehow you were given a second chance?

Would you be with the one, the one that you're with?

Or would you choose to be with somebody else?

Ok fear can keep you safe, I think we'd all agree with that

But is that how you'd want to feel, if you had the chance to go back?

So, at the end of the day, when you're lying in your bed

Do you hope, sometimes pray, you could be somewhere else instead?

Do you feel like you acted in haste, took a wrong turn and got lost?

Spending the rest of your life repenting and just counting the cost

DESTROY THE BOY

As a boy, I knew no concept of time

Which I now know gave me a liberty, a freedom

The future didn't exist

I took each day one day at a time

No plot, no plan, no agenda

My soul ambition was to find something exciting to do

It didn't matter to me whether the sky was grey, black or blue

I met every day with a smile and a dream of hidden treasure

As time went by, I realised the worlds intention was to destroy the boy

And everything he stood for and believed in

For the boy wasn't driven by money

The boy was colour blind

He only took what he needed

And truly understood the rationale and the feeling of community

The bond, the satisfaction in sharing

The boy spoke the truth, for his mind, heart and soul were not corrupted

They were all connected

What he saw, what he heard, what he felt, he took on board

He knew we were all unique, different, and special

But in reality, exactly the same

We all crave love and acceptance

Because whether your Muslim, Christian, Hindu or Sheikh,

We are all born with the righteous compass

To provide guidance when we are vulnerable, confused or weak

So you may ask yourself, why destroy the boy?

The answer to that question is quite simple

If you believe in God which most of us do

It's simple mathematics

There must be a devil too

To do what the devil's soldiers are here to do, destroy the boy

The child, the baby, a symbol of everything good in mankind

The vision our maker intended

Destroy the boy and the result will not be comprehended

DIVINE DESTINY

The destiny of our world,

Is in your hands

But there is no evil

Like the wickedness of man

So drop all your bombs

And shoot all your guns

You can't stop the life (love)

That shines from the sun

As strong as the lion

As large as the whale

It's the intemperance of man

Behind the reason we'll fail

And in our final hour

We'll shout who's to blame

But no man alive will escape

The burden of shame

27

That's when time and tide

Will return to the start

With the very first beat

From the love in my heart

And there by my side

My beautiful queen

And in the world that we share,

We will make love supreme

Together we'll erase

All the damage we've done

And every creeping, crawling, swimming,

flying, breathing, living thing will be as one

DREAMS ARE LIKE BLESSINGS

Promises and lies
Mistakes and successes
Orchestras and silhouettes
Words of love songs of sorrow
Wasted time, prayers for tomorrow
Stolen moments, dreams are like blessings
Future uncertain, past just keeps festering
It's the hope that will kill you
It's the love we all crave
Wish for strength and ambition
Wish that I could be brave
Everyday confronted by failure
Feel less than a man
With a life full of promise
In a world I don't understand
Everyone around me shares the pain in my heart
Meant to bring people together
I just tear them apart
If I were a sailor I'd take to the sea
If I were a doctor I'd cure my disease
If I were a lawyer I'd send myself to jail
If I were a postman I'd get lost in the mail
If I were a surgeon I'd cut out my heart
If I were a carpenter I'd make a new start

So tell me how many hours it takes, to break someone's
heart
How many years does it take to make your mark?
How many lifetimes does it take to live your dreams
Why do all the angels have to die to truly earn their wings?

EDEN

Songs of great sorrow, sounds of true joy

Words of passion and love, no man can destroy

Together we'll build a castle with a perimeter a million-foot high

Only the righteous may enter

They'll call this place Eden, Heaven on earth, the galaxy, the universes very centre

ELEPHANT

I can do anything, I can appear to be whoever I want

But when I'm at my best, my very best, I am the elephant

As crazy as it sounds not so long ago I was the snake

I couldn't stand up or admit to any of my mistakes

Disappeared in the grass the guilt and the shame became
too much for me to bear

So I shed my skin by the river that became a mirror

The riverbanks burst and overflowed with the pain from all
my own tears

At the bottom of the deep dark disillusion you granted me
one wish

My crossroads, a choice to choose, that's when I became a
fish

I swam for days, that became months-years were soon to
follow

No matter how far or fast I swam, I couldn't escape my
sorrow

A voice whispered to me, a command, you must now head
to shore for dry land

Through turbulent storms your love became my compass, my belief I began to understand

You were my father, my wonderful father and I'm my father's son

So as I rose up from the sea, took my first breath, I became the lion

And then I found my lioness, supreme in every way

I gave her my rib, my heart, my soul, then until this day

So now when I am at my best, surrounded by my young, I can be who or whatever I want

But time, life's experiences, good or bad, made me the elephant

EXISTENCE (EVERYTHING)

I wanna be the first, I wanna be the last

I wanna be everything in between

I want you in a glance

To feel my emotions

And in just one breath say what they all
mean

I never wanna feel you never listen

I never wanna feel I'm number two

I wanna be your reason life's worth living,

Your favourite thing in everything you do

You do so many things I need explaining,

I can't believe you just don't understand
your power

The effect you have over me every second of every minute
of every hour

Me, me, me, me, me all mine

From before the worlds existence

Until the very end of time

FEED THE FLAMES

As the pain washes over me

Takes control of me

Rips out the very soul of me

I rattle around in an empty shell

The deafening sound surrounding me

Confusing me

Swallowing me up

Chewing me up

Spitting me out

Abusing me

No respect for my feelings

No regrets for the torture

No remorse for the physical and mental slaughter

So who am I?

What are we?

Who am I?

35

What are we?

So where do you go from here?

Which way do I turn?

Go left so lost

Go right feel the burn

Choose burning, always choose burning

Choose the flames from the fire

They're so beautiful to me

Oh, so beautiful to see

As they flash and they flicker

As they eat away at me

Slowly destroying me

Now I understand I can at least find beauty in my pain

Such beauty in my tears

As I feed the flame

As I feed the flames

I see the pure beauty in my pain

As I feed the flames

I must feed the flames

Keep feeding the flames

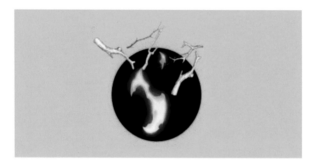

FEELS LIKE I'M LOSING IT

Sometimes it just feels like I'm losing it
Like I'm really losing it
Just losing it
Like I'm spending all my time trying to find it
Constantly reminded
I didn't really lose it
I threw it away
And that's the reason I'm acting this way
I can't bear waking up every day the fool
The man that had it all and lost it all
I didn't realise I found the rainbows end
My soul mate, my lover, my best friend
Most people can live their whole lives
And not even come close to finding someone like you
I let you slip away
Now I have to live with it and I can't live with it
I just can't believe it
I feel like I'm losing it

GOD SOON COME

So, called friends are my enemies, so called enemies are everywhere

They exist in a world of make believe, where all the people really don't care

Just keep moving forward, never look back

I am the future man, and that's a fact

Fortune misfortune, man they are both the same

Don't you know there's only one winner in this deadly game?

Trust in your heart baby, and nothing else

Leave all the nonbelievers alone on the shelf

For people are people, black, yellow or tan

God's rainbow created in his master plan

I ain't no gypsy fortune teller, I'm no voodoo man

Just waiting for revelations, I truly understand

Don't you know, don't you know, don't you know, we're all just living a dream

From birth to death, and everything in between

So, if you're out there listening, give me a shout

For you have twenty twenty vision, you know what life's about

And in the final hour, you will have no fear

Stood up straight at the pearly gates, you're finally here

God soon come

GOD'S FAVOURITE

I feel like I'm two people at war Charlie Charles
One person creative, the other destructive
One person caring, the other careless
One person strong and the other weak, you get the message
I'm sure
You know me better than most
I want desperately to be able to look at myself in the mirror
and like what I see
I believe I haven't done that for such a long time
I always feel my father's presence around me and I feel
ashamed and I know I'm letting him down
That feeling is truly unbearable
So here I am again Monday morning feeling like I need to
find the strength to overcome my demons
I know you probably don't believe me when I say, I was
put on this Earth for a purpose
I believe I was given a gift and a curse, in equal measure
My secret weapon is that I'm God's favourite
I just need to always remember that

GREEN GRASS

Didn't know I had it all, until I lost it

The grass seems so green

But now I'm faced with what could've been

They say it's better to have loved and lost, than never to
have loved at all

But you can't miss what you've never had and this feeling
feels so bad so bad

Long nights, short sight

Green grass

Blue moods, white lines

Green grass

They say there's no fool like an old fool

I gave your love away

I should have realised that love is the most precious jewel

I should have never ever gone astray

My mistakes my regrets buried in a shallow grave

Easy to uncover like the promises I made

Your heart broken, impossible to repair

And this feeling I just can't bear, just can't bear

Long nights, short sight

Green grass

Blue moods, white lines

Green grass

GUARANTEE

There are only a few things certain in life

There's no guarantees

Slave for what you want

What you want, you don't need

The first guarantee, we're all going to die

Guarantee number two

The first day you cry won't be the last day you cry

It doesn't matter if your black or white

Rich or poor

Able or disabled

Tom, Dick or Harry

Everybody on this earth has a cross they have to carry

Wealthier than people living in poverty

Choose the cowards way out

Hardship builds character

Those that have it all on a plate

Find the responsibility of the truth

Too much to contemplate

The third guarantee, the last guarantee well at least in my
opinion

HEAL ME

I don't know where to start

Or where this will end

So, called enemies so called friends

All here to remind me

That a love so bright just may blind me

Looks like lightning sounds like thunder

I can't believe the power of the spell she's put me under

And only you and you alone

Can truly feel me

Only you and you alone

Can truly heal me

Right now, right and wrong don't come into this

Have you ever felt a force you just can't resist?

A power so overwhelming

Witchcraft so spellbinding

Taking me over

Taking me over

Taking me over

And right now, I don't know if I'm in or out

My world my whole existence is left in doubt

My world in a spin

Can't believe the mess I find myself in

Only you and you alone

Can feel me

Only you and you alone

Can truly heal me

Truly heal me

Only you can heal me

Heal me

Heal me

Heal me

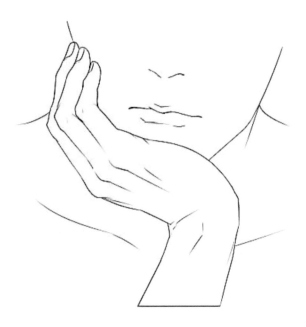

HOME (PART ONE)

He said I fell from the sky in the dark of the night
He said I spoke of another world, another place, the future,
it was the future

He said I knew that you wouldn't believe me, that you
didn't believe me

But I know deep inside you did, for had been there before
in your dreams, so you know it's true

I'm just here to remind you, I just came to remind you

I knew this day today I'd find you

Follow me, follow me dancing, tripping, flying though the
galaxy

For an eternity, yeah, an eternity, guided by the stars
without a single care, lighter than gravity

Yeah, he said I fell from the sky above, travelling at the
speed light, crashing through the clouds, just like lightning
with thunders might

Yeah with thunders awesome power, a force
uncompromising, leaving a trail of sparks so bright they
could almost blind you

But on his arrival, he gently whispered in my ear
I'm just here to remind you, I only came here to remind you

He said I knew you would forget home, yeah, I knew that
you would think that it was just a dream

You would eventually forget about me, forget about home

I'M GIVING IN

I'm giving in, I find it easier to take my last breath alone.

I'm giving in, what greater fear for me a life without hope.

I'm giving in, I just can't see the end of this misery.

I gave in the day you chose to walk out on me.

Left in a spin no direction now you're gone.

To tell the truth, I see no reason for me to carry on.

They say it's the worst of all sins to simply throw your life away.

Can't you see I've lost it all, there's just no need for me to stay.

I'm giving in, for that's the only thing I really have to left give.

A life without your love, is just no life for me to live.

I'm giving in, my heart as taken all that it can take.

Now giving in the last decision for me to make.

IF I NEVER SEE YOU AGAIN, WHAT GOES AROUND

I need to write down and try to unravel the situation I find myself in

The problem that I have with doing that is I just don't know where to begin

Okay, I'd like to think all my issues are about my relationship with my daughter, I say relationship I've not seen her for well over a year

She says she doesn't want to see me again, she says her decision is final and she has made her point crystal clear

I just can't seem to get my head around it, all this just seemed to come from out of the blue

I've tried to make things right, swallow my pride, I don't know what else I can do

I know I'll never win father of the year, I know I should have tried much harder

I should have used my dad as the example and tried to be a better father

No matter what I do or what I say the past is what it is

I'd hate to think that all the time we spent together, it's only pain I've left you with

I know mistakes, I've made so many, one thing I know for sure

You'll always be my little girl Hannah, and I couldn't love you more

Hand on my heart my life's a mess, and my problems run much deeper

What goes around comes around so now it's time I face the reaper

I really wish I could explain, without any excuses

The truth is I'm afraid of love for all my experiences of love were so cruel and so abusive

When I feel love my first instinct is to raise my guard

To love someone unconditionally I find impossible, because I'm just too scared

I know you are an adult, you can say and do as you chose

Just remember I truly love you Hannah, and if I never see you again that sweet love I'll never lose

So, I wish you luck and love in everything you do, whether you believe me or not Hannah I will always be here for you

IN THE DARKNESS

Away from the city lights

The only light is the sparkle in your eyes

Your heartbeat, the only sound

And it's my favourite sound

In the darkness when I hold you so tight

When it's just you and me,

In the darkness away from all those bright city lights

Just me and you holding hands

In the darkness

Watching our shadows dance across the wall

Oh this feeling when we're all alone

And we know there ain't anything in this world that can

harm us

There ain't anything in this world that can destroy us

There ain't anything in this universe stronger than us

We are unbreakable, unstoppable and this love power we

share

Yeah we share

In the darkness, just you and me holding hands

Holding hands

Without a sound

Oh so quiet all around us

Just the sound of our hearts

The sound of our hearts beating

When I hold you so tight

In the darkness

Nothing can do us any harm

Just you and me in the darkness

IT'S ALL ABOUT YOU

Sometimes don't you know before you rise?
You have to fall
Remember, there ain't no day time without the night time
Complain about the rain
Always praying for the sunshine
There's beauty in everything you do
There's wonder in everything you see
Immerse yourself in your reality
For there really ain't any future
Or past, there's only right now
And every lemon is your lemonade
Of that I have no doubt
Spread love
Make that your own ambition
Start living your dreams,
Instead of always wishing
Cos believe it or not, it's always about you
Don't be afraid, be brave in all you try to do
For you know you only truly fail
If you never try
Coz once you start believing
That's when you'll truly fly

IT'S A JUNGLE

It's all about survival, it's a jungle out there

My name ain't Tarzan and I don't swing through the trees

But every animal you can imagine shares these urban streets

Just like the jungle, there's a hierarchy everyone knows their position

No one steps over the line, for around here that's a life or death decision

First rule, don't mess with the lions that goes without saying

The monkeys tried that once, I soon found out them guys just ain't playin

IT'S EASY TO SAY

Looking back trying to figure out where I went wrong
Yeah keep looking back, always singing the same song
Over and over again
Over and over again
I realise now that it's easier said
It's easy to say
Much harder to do
Now I know just what I put you through
It's much easier to say
Much harder to do
I only realise now what I put you through
And if I could only turn back the hands of time
I'd hold you tight, so tight you'd read my mind
But it's easy to say
Much harder to do
So now I spend every day
Every night, all alone, feeling blue
Oh those long miss you nights
So many miss you nights
Oh those miss you nights
So many miss you nights
Alone and crying
It's easier to say
Much harder to do
And it's only now I realise

The pain and the heartache I put you through
The pain and the heartache I put you through
Oh but it's easier to say
So much harder to do

IT'S THE WAY GOD PLANNED IT

Why do some creatures walk, whilst others fly?

Why do the unrighteous live whilst the worthy die?

I don't understand it it's just the way God planned it.

Why do so many children have no food to eat?

Why does a man's life journey end with him sleeping on the street?

I don't understand it maybe it's the way God planned it.

Why do innocent children get abused?

Why do winners win and losers lose?

I don't understand it it's just the way God planned it.

Why do we have to work and work so hard?

Whilst the wealthy disrespect and disregard.

I don't understand it it's just the way God planned it.

Why do grown people become slaves to addiction?

Instead of the love of life and true conviction.

I don't understand it must be the way God planned it.

Why is this world that we live in built on lies?

And we are immune to the sound of a baby's cries.

I don't understand it it's just the way God planned it.

Why is the quest for wealth our only goal?

Why don't we all repent and save our souls?

I don't understand it it's just the way God planned it.

Why don't we all believe and give love a try?

For the beautiful truth is we all will die.

I don't understand it it's just the way God planned it.

KISS YOU GENTLY

I'll pick you up
I'll kiss you gently
I'll pick you up
I'll kiss you so gently
I'll take care of you
I'll do anything you ask me to
Yeah I'll pick you up
And I'll show you off
And at the end of the night
I'll kiss you gently
So gently
At the end of the night
When we are all alone
I'll wrap my arms around you
And I'll kiss you gently
So gently
And you know I'll never do you wrong
I'll never let you down
And I won't ever fool around
Yeah I'll put my arms around you
And I'll kiss you gently
Yeah put my loving arms around you
And kiss you gently

Oh you're the girl of my dreams

You're everything to me
Truly heaven sent to me
And that's why I'll kiss you gently

LEAVE IT ALONE

Devil reign and he's reigning right now
Killing my dreams and the child right now
Making me believe I'm sitting on the top of the world
But he's a magician he's got me fooled, he's got me
believing
Stealing my ambition, taking my enthusiasm
His lies, they've cut me to the bone
Turning my righteous heart into solid stone

Now I can't leave it alone
Now I can't stop
I need to stop
Why can't I leave it alone?
I just can't stop

If you saw him in the day time
You would cross over to the other side of the road
Coz he's a mother ticking bomb and he's about to explode
He's going to light the fuse
He's going to blow up the world
Yes he's going to light the fuse
He's going to blow up the world

I didn't realise the grave danger until he was right there in
my own home
By that time it was far too late
I've seen how he operates

When I was young, he operated underground
Now when you look on every corner
He can be found

Now I can't leave it alone
I can't leave it alone
I need to leave it alone
I'm addicted
It's like I'm addicted
I must be addicted
I can't leave it alone
Can't leave it alone
I can't leave it alone
I can't stop
I can't leave it alone
When I need to leave it alone
I need to stop
I need to stop

When I was a youth I used to burn Cali weed
Now the devil lurks on every corner
You now the devil lurks on every corner
I need to leave it alone

LET IT BURN

Don't worry about it
Stop worrying about losing it
Because the truth is, you didn't really have it in the first
place
And by the way, you can't lose what you never had
So cut out the drama, there is no need to act sad
This is a game you can't win
Sometimes you've just got to let it go
Let it burn
Yes sometimes you've just got to let it go
Let it burn
Let it burn
Let it burn
Let it burn

There's no point wasting all of your emotions
Always fearing that you're losing it
But I'm telling you, you can't lose what you never had
So forget all about the drama
Let's sit around the fire, feel the flames
And let it burn
Let it burn
Let it burn
Let it burn
Let it burn

Coz sometimes you've just got to let go of something you
didn't really own
Let go of something that was never really yours
See the beauty in the flames, the heat of the flames
Yeah bid it fun, fair well

Let it burn

Let it burn

Let it burn

Let it burn

See the beauty in the flames

Let it go

Find the beauty in the flames

There's so much beauty in the flames

Yeah you've just got to let it go

Let it go

Let it go

Let it go

Let it go

Find the flames

LET IT GROW

I remember being alone in the dark

I can still feel the pain time and time again

I can't remember ever feeling a touch that was warm or
tender

All my thoughts of love or hope just surrendered

Just surrendered

But where love is planted deep in your heart

It cannot be taken, destroyed or broken

Sometimes you may feel all hope is gone

But love will never leave you

Please be strong, just stay strong

Maybe this is just fate

Or maybe it's just destiny

Maybe this is just a reason

Like the changing of the seasons

Maybe this is your destiny

A reason just like the changing of the seasons

Sometimes you may feel all hope is gone

But love never leaves you

Please be strong,

For love is the force that spins the world

And you were chosen

Let love grow

Let grow

Please let it grow

Let love grow

Let it grow

LEAD BY EXAMPLE

Your children need a hero, an example to follow

Showing them the way to a brighter tomorrow

So, when you look in the mirror, tell me what do you see?

A child with a beard looking straight back at me

So, what do I need to do to change my situation?

Pray to the Lord for my sweet soul salvation

But not after every prayer you can say Amen

Sometimes you need to find the strength and the courage
from deep within

So, don't let my last breath be the cries of a sinner

What's in the cat is in the kitten, like my father I'm a winner

LIFE GOES ON

I took your love for granted

Thought the love was sweeter on the other side

So, I broke it and it stayed broken

Your love for me just died

And all my promises regrets and sorry-full excuses

I can't cover all my lies

Coz the love wasn't sufficient on the other side

Now the heart ache that I'm feeling I just can't hide

Coz you really don't know what you've got until it's gone

And the world keeps turning,

Life goes on

LIFE'S ILLUSION

How do you eat an elephant?

One spoon at a time

So how do you drink the ocean?

Tell the people that it's wine

For everything you see around you is simply an illusion

Promises and lies you're fed, just add to the confusion

If, for just one day we were told the truth

That would not be the solution

In fact, I think it's safe to say

The truth would start a revolution

We're spoon fed information

For knowledge and wisdom is the power

The tools to make unworthy, wealthy tumble from the tower

They say the first will be the last, and all that

Maybe there's some truth in that

But when I look through my history books

It doesn't apply if your skin is black

I don't want to come across all negative

There ain't a chip on this shoulder

But positivity is a coat you wear when the truth is so much colder

LOVE

I know you're really bored right now and you need
something to do

You feel you are put on this earth for a reason, what this
reason is you've not got a clue

You say you feel you've no direction, no purpose, dreams
or goals

Where you'll end up you say is a mystery you just can't
seem to take control

You tell me you feel empty like somebody stole your
ambition, like no matter where you are you're lost

The loneliest place is when there is no place where you
belong

The secret ingredient, a man needs a soul mate, it's the love
from a good woman that makes a man feel strong

Maybe your destiny is to live a life of frustration, with
unanswered questions that will haunt you till your very
last day

Should you accept your fate? Convince yourself that it was meant to be this way?

It's hard to fight and believe in something you don't know exists or that you've never even seen

You need to close your eyes, completely drop your guard and let blind faith help you truly let go

For its then and only then that you'll find what you spent a life time searching for

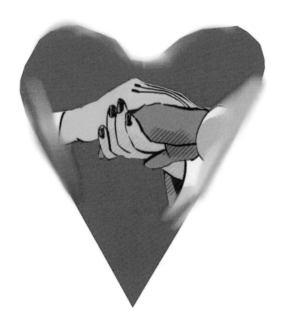

MAYBE THIS TIME WE'LL MAKE IT

Yeah, maybe this time we'll make it
Yeah maybe this time we'll go all the way
But just for now, let's try to make it through another day
Let's not get too ambitious, let's just go one step at a time
Because the past tells me, we just don't know where to
draw the line
Baby, you know when we fall, we fall from the highest high
And when we hit the ground, it sounds like thunder and
lightning fills the sky
But when we make up, there's no greater feeling
I almost feel like I could fly
I know we're so different, grizzly and polar bears
There's no point me trying to change
I know you feel the same
Polar bears and grizzlies but we carry the same last name
Close your eyes for a second, imagine your life without me
Yeah it's scary ain't it baby, that second felt like an eternity

MY GIRL

I told my girl I feel your pain
I truly believed she'd feel the same
But I find myself ten million miles from that
Walking a tightrope like an acrobat
Like a slot machine, what you put in you don't necessarily
get out
I found out a little bit too late, that's what life's about
I thought if you felt love so strong, she must feel the same
That just shows my inexperience playing the love game
I'd like to think my father didn't raise a fool
But love like life can be so cruel
Never the less, it's faith and hope that drives me
And destiny says love will one day find me

MY GIRL ON THE SWINGS

I had a dream about my girl on a swing

On a sunny day in Spring

It saved me, it truly saved me

I found that I had somehow lost my way

I needed to remember my destination

This situation why I was sent here

I know I'm being tested everyday a mission

I was given tools to help me find my way back home

Eyes to see, a mouth to whisper and ears to listen

I know at best I can be the wisest fool, and at my worst a clown

So many put their faith in me, I'm so afraid can't let them down

For all my many faults God knows I try God knows I try

For even on my darkest days, I never cry, protest or complain

When my times are brightest I react exactly the same

Some people spend their entire life in the pursuit of fortune and wealth

Their time would be much better spent searching for knowledge of self

Every question answered the truth so clear

The truth is power accompanied by the fear

I saw that money was undoubtedly the root of all evil

It made demons and non-believers of righteous people

I thought about my girl on a swing

On a warm day in Spring

The vision took the fear away, and brought order to my dismay

It truly saved me, yes it saved me

At that moment gave me something to believe in

A new direction for me to strive for and to stand for

I found a reason to live for and something worth dying for

In just one second all the wonders of the world were revealed

Love was at the heart of every question, riddle or mystery

The trick is never look forward for the answers lie in our
history

The words the paint, music the canvas, the beat our hearts,
rhythm the dancers

So on judgment day when total chaos going off

I'll close my eyes and think happy thoughts

My girl on the park, pushing her on a swing

On a warm sunny day in the middle of Spring

It will save me, it will truly save me

ONLY GOD CAN JUDGE US

I got some good luck so I put it in my pocket

Because you know when you need it you just can't find it

And you know bad luck goes without saying it's
guaranteed

You need to work through that stuff if you want to succeed

Stay positive ride it like surfing a wave

Sometimes you have to find the strength for the struggle
could be years' months or days

Remember first place for you is last place for many others,
that's why the truth is only god can judge us

ONLY YOU AND YOU ALONE

When I fall will you catch me?

When I'm tired will you carry me?

When I'm in danger, will you protect
me?

When I'm consumed in misery and sadness, will you
comfort me?

When I'm confused and uncertain about my future, will
you reassure me?

When I'm flat broke, not a penny to my name, will you
support me?

When my beliefs and opinions conflict with yours, will you
respect my diversity?

When I grow old, and do not have the ability to look after
myself, will you care for me?

When the reaper comes to claim my soul, will you look him
in the eyes and shun him?

Will you pray for me?

Please pray for me

PAPER PLANE

It may fly for a while but comes crashing down time and time again

Don't ever try to board this paper plane, it never leaves the ground

Me just like a paper plane, ain't safe to be around

Who is the greatest fool? The fool? Or the one that follows

Life Living day to day, no thoughts, no cares about tomorrow's

Always treating everyday like summer is the only season

No direction, no dreams, almost nothing to believe in

Spinning round and round like autumn leaves falling from the trees

There ain't a sadder thing I've seen, than a man living on his knees

PRAY FOR ME

So I went to see my mother
I ain't seen her for a while
I know that she has other children
But she told me I was her favourite child
I told her I'm in trouble
I'm a sinner not a saint
And this picture on my canvas
Ain't a pretty picture that I paint
Mother, mother pray for me
Mother, pray for me

I need someone in my corner
Someone to rescue me
So I went down the road to see my sister
She put her arms around me
When she looked me in my eyes
She saw the desperation
She said, do you know what she's gonna pray for me
Yeah, she said she's gonna
She told me she's gonna pray for me

I need someone, anyone in my corner
Someone to rescue me
Save my soul
Save my soul
Save my soul
Pick up the phone

Pick up the phone
So I call my brother,
I said 'brother I need your help'
Oh this situation,
I need you to pray for me

REGRETS

A life of regrets I have so many

A millionaire I would be if each were a penny

As I now look back and reflect on my past endeavours

Never put dedication or hard work before sinful pleasures

Tomorrow became my signatory tune

Now just like my life it's all over too soon

All I do with my time is dream of what I could have
become

Feels like I'm living my life through the eyes of my sons

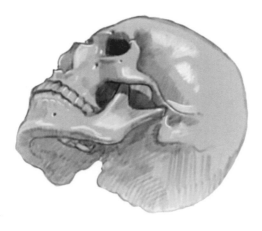

SHOULDN'T THAT BE YOU

When I'm all alone and need someone to turn to.

When I'm so afraid and don't know what to do.

When my world feels like it's crumbling around me.

When confusion, disillusion.

When this memory is the first that I remember.

My first thought I cling onto.

When I try my best to be the person you can rely on.

Change nightmares into dreams.

Stop living in the past.

Horrific thoughts they never ever leave me.

Not kill any hope or chance for this to last.

I've now turned into someone I can't face in the mirror.

It used to be the dark, but it's the light I fear.

I understand now light is life and there stands my conflict.

When the only tool you have is a hammer.

Everything becomes a nail.

And if you never ever change that situation.

No matter what you do in life you're sure to fail.

Dish out wisdom, words of advice just like confetti.

So why is it everything I do seems to go wrong?

It feels like everyone around me is always singing,

I just don't know the lyrics to the song.

SLAVE

I'll tell you something for nothing, my Dad would turn in his grave

If he knew one day his favourite Son would end up as a slave

But the really scary thing is I believe my father knows

And it's casting a shadow in my life, everywhere I go

I don't know who I pray to more, my father or the Lord

It just feels like neither one is listening, as if I'm being ignored

The funny thing about my situation, my Dad would always say

If you don't hear you will feel, and it's turned out that way

SLIPPERY SLOPE

My dad called it the slippery slope

But I just didn't listen

Then I realised too late

That drug stuff is designed to kill ambition

Now I look at my life broken in tatters

I destroyed all the precious things in my world that really mattered

SORRY

If sorry was a bucket it would have a great big hole in the bottom

Unlike before it used to be sturdy trustworthy, now it's useless I let a good thing get rotten

You don't understand the bucket's importance, or recognise its value

For the bucket symbolises your morals, a compass for everything you do

SUCCESS

Success means many things to many people

So listen close, this is the truth, we're all equal

What I am about to say is more than essential

It is what everybody needs to reach their true potential

I hope when you read this it all makes sense

And it gives you the incentive to jump off the fence

0-9 never 1-10, if I have your attention let me begin

The first step is 0 and that's all that you're worth

If you don't heed the basic instructions before leaving earth

Step 1 - is respect that you should have for oneself

If you live without this, you'll respect no one else

Step 2 - realise the value of time

To waste this commodity is more than a crime

Step 3 - No matter who wrongs you, show them love

Always remember hate never did any good

Step 4 - is your gift, your purpose your goal

The secret of this lies deep in your soul

Step 5 - Life is a test, don't lose the big picture

In times of great weakness, revelations the scripture

Step 6 - be prepared for much hardship in the quest of what you believe

Stand tall, never waver you're sure to succeed

Step 7 - is most important- Learn to follow your feelings

They'll never lead you wrong once you have learned their true meanings

Step 8 - Always start with the foundation, put in the floor before working on the ceiling

Life's experiences whether good or bad, are all character building

Step 9 - maybe the most important on this list

The quest for the truth

That's why we exist

SWITCHING LANES

I don't know where I'm going

But I know where I've been

You know I've seen such trouble

So much trouble I have seen

One eye on the future, trying to leave the past

Become the ship that's sinking

And now I'm sinking fast

I've tried to run from problems, but I just can't escape

Think what I could have done different, but it's just a bit
just a little bit too late

Now with great responsibilities, I know that I must change

Slow down, check my mirrors it's time for switching lanes

I don't think I'm a bad man, maybe a little mischievous

Some say insanity and madness are just the flip-side to incredible genius

I truly feel there is a point, a reason for my life and my existence

One day I'll realise the truth, my love will make the difference

TALK TO ME

Talk to me,
Tell me who I'm supposed to be
Why are you afraid of me?
When did I become bad company?
For everything I've ever done
I did for you
And for every time I let you down
I cried for you
Talk to me
Explain to me
Help me see the man I'm supposed to be
The man I'm supposed to be
I know I'm far from perfect
I'm kind of strange in a weird way
Yeah, but I'm telling you the truth
With my hand on my heart
I'll love you till my dying day
Till my dying day
Just talk to me
Help me realise the changes
The difference between a friend and enemy
Oh tick tock, tick tock
All I hear is tick tock, tick tock
Time running out
Running out
Running out

Running out

Oh the sound in my head goes tick tock, tick tock

The sound of the clock

My time is running out

You walking out

Me left in doubt

Talk to me

THE LADDER THEORY

Step 1: To acknowledge that there is a ladder

Step 2: To establish your position on the ladder right now

Step 3: Trying to imagine what the top of the ladder looks like to you

Step 4: Ask yourself the question, if you want to be at the top of the ladder and if not where you want to be on the ladder?

Step 5: Are you willing to do whatever you need to do to achieve your desired position on the ladder?

Step 6: Always remember there are pros and cons to all positions on the ladders, so think about the consequences to the position

Step 7: If you are willing to accept the downfalls think of an action plan

Step 8: Completely commit to the steps you have worked through and climb the ladder

Step 9: When you have reached your goal, your dream position, on the ladder, ask yourself, am I happier now or was I happier before I embarked on this journey

Step 10: If the answer to Step 9 is yes, you must have found love and contentment on your journey, your climb
If you're answer is no, please repeat the whole process Step 1, for Love must be the pinnacle of every human's journey
It's the only real reason we still exist

THE LIGHT

I used to be afraid of the darkness

I hated all the shadows around me

I used to feel that deep in my heart

Someone special was destined to come and find me

But really, I have always been a dreamer

Hope standing side by side with ambition

Or maybe sometimes just foolish pride

Is there any harm in this little boy wishing? I feel now that
I've reached a crossroads

I need to choose my next destination

It feels like I've been stuck here for years

So, scared I'm just waiting and waiting

Cos now I realise it's the light that I fear

In the light is when people can judge me

In the light, you can see all my faults

The lowest of the low, all above me

My father always told me never worry

You'll always get to where your meant to be

Sometimes I can sense him looking down on me from
heaven

Like on earth, his love guiding me

THE BUTTERFLY THEORY

I remember when I spoke with an angel's soul

But my love and kindness turned into control

The trust I was given slipped through my hands

When the needs of another didn't meet my demands

I abused the gift

You gave to my heart

Now a million steps forward, you'll find me back at the start

You told me to pull, I questioned I pushed

And the world's greatest treasures

Returned back to dust

All God's creatures retreat from the Sun

For they truly know the damage I've done

They hide in the shadows awaiting their fate

But the fool becomes king for love conquers hate

102

THE LOVE GAME

Theirs a game I know that we all play

Some play all the time, but we all end up playing one day

The rules are very easy, quite simple to understand

But just like life, the end results may not turn out as you
planned

The stakes are high but the rewards are great

I do recommend before you start the game, check what's on
your plate

Cos, believe it or not both players often lose unlike in many
games

For the chances, you take the choices you make, the end
results the same

So, take heed before playing the love game, don't rush in in
search of lust or just pleasure

There's much more to love so don't be the fool who repents
at his own leisure

WAR - WE'RE ALL RESPONSIBLE

Question? What are your priorities?

Always remember life is not a battle, it's a war

Every day you will face challenges

These challenges are sent to test you, to make you stronger

So when you are faced with problems, issues or difficult
decisions you have to make

Learn to trust your heart.

For most decisions revolve around love or money

The wisest man who walked this earth, and beyond

A man that lived an eternity, a man who witnessed many
amazing things

A man who suffered incredible injustices and unbearable
loss

A man who would overcome prejudice, hate and hideous
boundaries barriers put before him

A man who when he spoke it was alive, but the sweetest
whisper the purest truth

His words were meant for every man, woman and child
He told them all, money is the root of all evil

That love truly spins the world, but we chose not to listen

So please remember, life is more than a battle, it's a war

If you make the wrong choices and decisions, you stand to lose everything.

Follow your heart to find a beautiful death

For only God can judge your life, but we all must die

Black, white, rich poor, man, woman or child

This is what you are fighting for, for only you can find a beautiful death

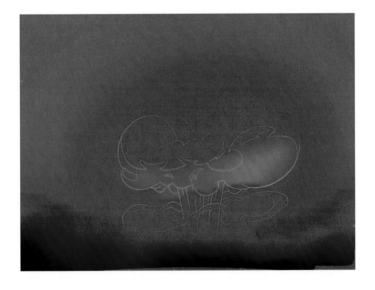

WHEN LOVE COMES CALLING

When you feel the love come calling

Let it in, don't pretend you don't know

There's a place for this emotion, open your heart and let it grow

I can tell by your expression love has called here before

But you felt so uncertain that you closed the door

You hold on to your past with a vice like grip

Don't watch your step

Run little girl

You won't slip

You'll travel so fast your arms will become wings

Please don't question your heart, for this is when life begins

For just one question, and one question alone

Will turn your heart and your wings into stone

So when love comes calling trust in your soul.

Let the wonderful feeling of love take control

If you want all that shines, you must give it your all

If you think of your position, you are certain to fall

If you lose your faith and fall from above

Don't cry little girl

You can't stop the love

THE PERFECT STAR

The perfect star has seven points

Each one has a purpose

To reveal the secret of each point

You must dig deep beneath the surface

Persevere and you will find

Each characteristic mirrors your own

For everyone who walks this earth is guided by a perfect
star no one walks alone

You may find all this hard to believe you may not
understand it

When surrounded by the wickedness of mankind

Guess that's the way God planned it

Acknowledgments

This book and the poems within it are the product of the support and guidance I received throughout my life, in honour of that I would like to give a special mention to the following people for all they have done for me personally and for the charity Harmony Youth Project.

Firstly, I want to thank my parents. My father Wesley George Barrett for his guidance, encouragement and love. Before he passed in 2010 he used to say to me, "Do you know how I know my life has been a success? Me knowing none of my children will have to go through what I had to go through." And my mother Delores Barrett, who is always there for me with unconditional love and support. She is my rock, the foundation of my family and losing my dad made me realise even more so her strength, even though at this present time she has dementia and is struggling every day to be herself she is still the strongest person I know. When my father would talk about her he would say "It doesn't matter what I do for you, how long I do it and how long I live. I could never do for you what your mother has done for you in your life."

I would also like to mention Hanif Ali, my first and constant mentor. The first person besides my parents to believe in me, to back me to the hilt and support me not just with his words but with his actions. He saw something special in me that I never saw, his wisdom is unbelievable and to this day he is the only man as close in guidance as my father was to me. There would be no Harmony Youth Project without Hanif and my journey and life would be completely different.

And Denise Luczka, I met her because of Hanif's influence and I am forever grateful I did. Denise's influence on me was very different from Hanif, he and I were of similar backgrounds and ages but Denise was from a very different background. She helped me analyse and understand my actions, why they worked and recognise the theory behind why they were successful, which gave me a complete overview of every situation or practice that I delivered during my many diverse work experiences. The biggest credit I could give her is that she taught me the importance of reflection. I will be forever grateful for that because it has stuck and it is a massive thing to learn and I still use it now, on a daily basis in my journal, professionally and personally.

I'd like to give a special mention to John Hynes, who I met around ten years ago, in 2012. As soon as I met him, it felt like I'd already known him for most of my life, I felt so at ease with him. He showed a genuine interest in what our organisation does, it wasn't too long before I asked if he would be a trustee for Harmony Youth Project. It was only two years later, in 2014 that he became our Chairman. I wanted to give John a special mention for two reasons, the first being when John got involved with Harmony Youth Project we had been going through some financial difficulties, his involvement brought amazing business expertise, financial management and a progressive and innovative way to develop the charity. His business associates and influences helped with funding and our direction as a whole. The second reason is that over the last ten years, I've got to know John on a really personal level, and I truly admire him. I've seen him at work, how he treats his staff, how he treats everyone he comes into contact with, with respect and honesty. I requested that he become chairman because of his leadership qualities. I have become very close to and respect his family, especially his wife, Paula. Over the years, I've seen him in the role of husband and father to his children. I believe in every aspect and every situation John leads by example and therefore he has become a fantastic role model for me and I believe since I've met him I have become a far better man for his influence.

Lastly but in no way least, I want to thank all the people I have been so fortunate to meet and work with during my journey into further education, youth work, counselling and Harmony Youth Project. Those people who have helped me build, develop and love the charity I've been involved with for the past 21 years. I never want to give the impression I did this alone, I've always had a group of people who were passionate, creative, loyal and innovative to back me. Without them, there would be no Harmony Youth Project and no book.

https://www.harmonyyouthproject.co.uk

All the funds raised by the sale of this book are going directly to Harmony Youth Project, children's charity and the development of a young people's counselling service to reach more of those in need and continue our positive work within our community.

Sincere thanks to Mr John Hynes (Copy Print Services Ltd), Mr Tony Hayes (Diamond Solutions UK Ltd), Natalie Matthews, Charity Liaison Manager (JD Foundation) and Traci Corrie, Chair (JD Foundation), for their support in this book.

Published in 2022 by
Preeta Press, Bolton,
Greater Manchester

preetapress.com

Illustrations by Blake Ugo-Ogbonna

ISBN: 978-1-9196344-1-8

Printed by Imprintdigital.com